FIRST STEPS IN SCIENCE

WHAT IS MATTER?

A FOREST ADVENTURE!

BY KAY BARNHAM AND MARCELO BADARI

First published in Great Britain in 2023
by Wayland
Copyright © Hodder and Stoughton, 2023

Editor: Grace Glendinning
Cover design concept: Peter Scoulding
Cover and inside design: Emma DeBanks

HB ISBN: 978 1 5263 2017 9
PB ISBN: 978 1 5263 2016 2

Printed and bound in China

Wayland, an imprint of
Hachette Children's Group
Part of Hodder and Stoughton
Carmelite House
50 Victoria Embankment
London EC4Y 0DZ

An Hachette UK Company
www.hachette.co.uk
www.hachettechildrens.co.uk

We recommend adult supervision at all times while completing the activity in this book. Children should always be supervised when working with reactive materials. Some of the ingredients in the activity may contain allergens. Anyone with a known allergy must avoid these.

MIX
Paper from
responsible sources
FSC® C104740
FSC
www.fsc.org

The website addresses (URLs) included in this book were valid at the time of going to press. However, it is possible that contents or addresses may have changed since the publication of this book. No responsibility for any such changes can be accepted by either the author or the Publisher.

WHAT IS MATTER?

Let's find out! Join our super-robots as they trek through the trees. We'll have great fun in the forest and learn cool facts about matter, too. Let's go, super-scientists!

Bolt, Pixel and Jet love to be outdoors.

Today, they are going to follow a nature trail through the forest. They will be on the lookout for babbling brooks and colourful plants. They will enjoy the fresh air.

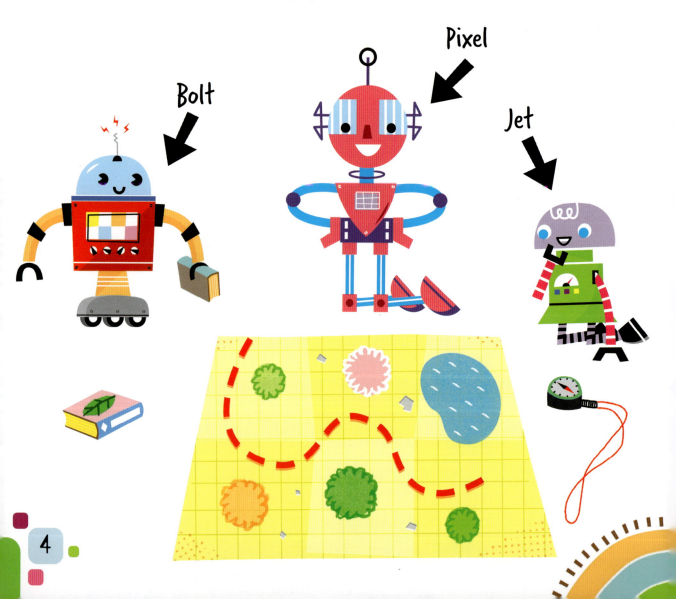

Bolt

Pixel

Jet

4

How many amazing things do you think the super-robots will see and do during their forest adventure?

It's time to go! The robots travel to the forest by super-**magnetic** robot train. They whizz past houses and parks.

Did you know that if something takes up space, it's called **matter**?

Even me?

They zoom through tunnels and race over bridges. They see so many things on the way.

Even you!

The super-robots arrive at the forest at last. Pixel, Bolt and Jet gaze at the beautiful trees, with their leaves of red, green and gold.

This place is SO COOL.

This backpack is SO HEAVY.

Pixel and Jet look inside Bolt's rucksack.
Bolt has brought:

collection jars

fizzy robot juice

YUM!
YUM!

a multi-tool
gadget

solar-powered
chargers
(for charging
super-robots'
batteries)

nuts and bolts
(robot snacks
to keep them up
and running!)

a hover-umbrella

a jet-fuel robot
camping stove

an iron
saucepan

It's ALL matter!

And each bit of the matter, from the juice to the jet-fuel, is made of tiny parts called **atoms**. They are far too small to see without a powerful **microscope** (unless you're a super-robot).

With my magnify-eyes I can see atoms just like a microscope can! Check it out!

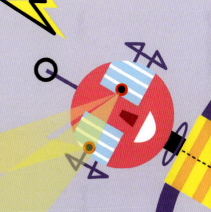

Let's go and find some more matter!

one iron atom

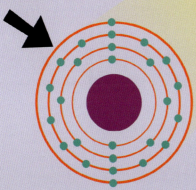

Pixel, Bolt and Jet set off. They switch on their super-stretching legs to move FAST along the trail!

They **LEAP** over rocks.

They **HOP** over puddles and streams.

The wind BLOWS across their faces.

Matter can be a **solid**,
a **liquid** or a **gas**. These are
called the **states of matter**. Which
state of matter is a rock,
a stream or the wind?

Soon, the forest trail becomes steeper.
Pixel, Jet and Bolt climb up and up
and up.

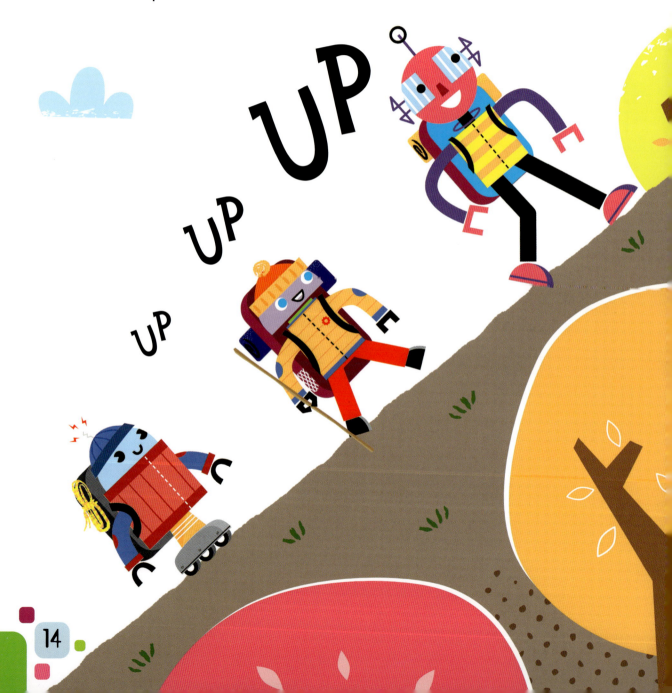

The super-robots are getting tired and hungry. It's time to take a break and have a snack.

The crunchy, solid nuts and bolts are REALLY yummy. Pixel uses her magnify-eyes to look at them up close.

This is a very big picture of tightly packed atoms.

15

As they explore near their resting spot, the super-robots are happy to find a cool, liquid waterfall.

Atoms in a liquid can move freely about. This allows liquids to flow and change shape.

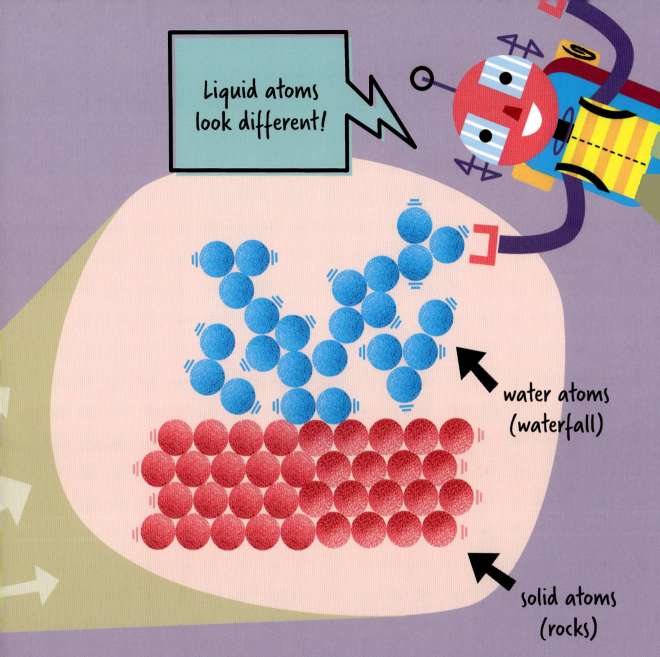

Liquid atoms look different!

water atoms (waterfall)

solid atoms (rocks)

Pixel's magnify-eyes show that there is much more space between liquid atoms than solid atoms!

Filled with energy, Pixel, Jet and Bolt follow the nature trail right to the top of the mountain. What a view!

The super-robots feel the cool mountain air. Air is a mixture of gases – the third state of matter.

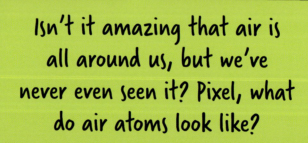

Isn't it amazing that air is all around us, but we've never even seen it? Pixel, what do air atoms look like?

Pixel switches on her magnify-eyes
again and zooms in on the air.
Will the atoms be invisible?

I can see air atoms!
There's a lot of space between
them ... They are moving fast
in all directions!

Just then, the Sun comes out from behind the clouds! Suddenly, it's very hot. Thank goodness Jet has brought a small cooler box with her. (Even super-robots like ice lollies!)

Yay!

Yay!

Yay!

Oh, no! The ice lollies are dripping ... The three super-robots slurp the lollies very, very quickly before they melt fully in the hot sunshine.

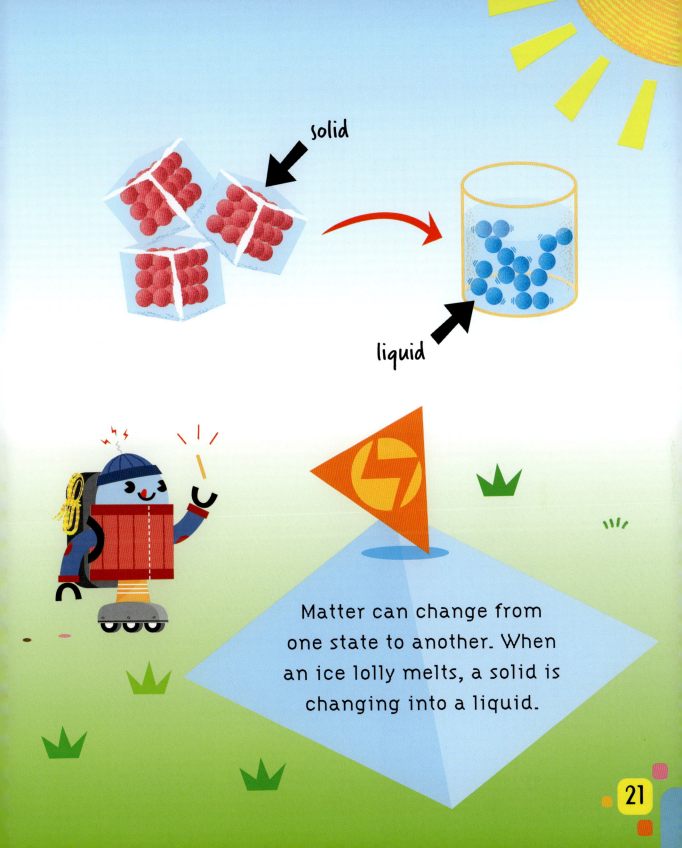

solid

liquid

Matter can change from one state to another. When an ice lolly melts, a solid is changing into a liquid.

Who wants a bowl of nuts-and-bolts porridge before we head back? I can warm it up quickly with my stove and pan!

Me!

Me!

Bolt fills his saucepan with water and turns on the camping stove. The super-robot jet flames soon make the water bubble and boil, ready to cook porridge.

When water boils, it changes into an invisible gas called **water vapour**. This is another example of matter changing from one state to another. Here, a liquid changes into a gas.

water vapour

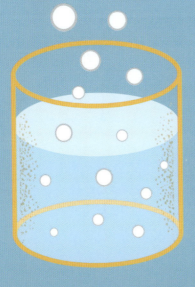

Full and happy, it's time for the robots to make the trek back to the train.

23

The lollies in the sun melted quickly in the heat. And the water boiled super-robot-fast on the stove. But sometimes matter changes v-e-r-r-r-r-r-y s-l-o-w-l-y.

Water from this mountain stream is s-l-o-w-l-y rising, atom by atom from the surface of the water.

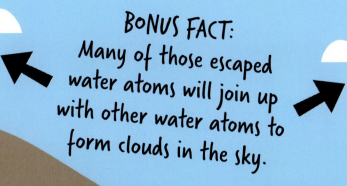

BONUS FACT:
Many of those escaped water atoms will join up with other water atoms to form clouds in the sky.

When heaps of leaves sit for a long time, the leaves are no longer leaves at all! They are wet sludge.

When matter changes into something else altogether, this is called a **chemical change**.

(See page 28 to try out your own exciting chemical change!)

Before they catch the train, Pixel, Jet and Bolt look at the treasures they have collected on their trip.

Pixel has a jar of colourful and shiny rocks. They are VERY heavy.

Jet's jar carries water from the waterfall. It weighs less than the rocks.

Bolt's jar contains nothing but fresh mountain air! It's the lightest jar of all.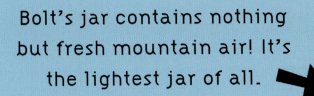

The more atoms that are squished into matter, the more **dense** it is and the more it weighs.

And now it's time to go home. The super-robots have had an awesome day in the forest!

You can explore more ways to change matter FAST with some common ingredients in your kitchen. It's time for science in action!

Make a bottle volcano

WARNING: even super-scientists must have the help of an adult for this activity!
Do this outside or in the safety of a bath tub!

1 Mix the bicarbonate of soda, the washing-up liquid and the water in a bowl.

2 Use the funnel to pour the mixture into the bottle.

3 Pour the vinegar into the bottle too.

Whoosh!

Whoosh!

4 Sit back and watch your bottle volcano erupt from the top of the bottle!

Mixing some different types of matter together makes a super-fast chemical change.

GLOSSARY

Atom: the tiniest part of matter

Chemical change: when one substance combines with another substance to from a new substance

Dense: when lots of atoms are squished together

Gas: a state of matter containing atoms that whizz quickly about

Liquid: a state of matter containing atoms that move freely

Magnetic: when an object has particular atoms that make it attract certain other objects to itself

Matter: anything that takes up space, such as a lunch box, fruit juice or air

Microscope: a device used to look at very small things so that they appear much bigger

Solid: a state of matter containing atoms so close together that they hardly move

States of matter: the different types of matter – solid, liquid or gas

Water vapour: a gas made of water atoms

GUIDE FOR TEACHERS, PARENTS AND CARERS

This book can help young children to learn about matter – one of the concepts that form the foundation of physics. They may then begin to understand how the world and everything in it works.

Matter is something that takes up space. It can exist in different states, which have different properties. Matter can change states, too.

In this book, readers observe the different types of matter in real life, through the eyes of super-robot friends. They may then go on to discover new examples for themselves.

PLEASE NOTE: this book contains an activity that requires adult supervision and help, including possible allergens.

FURTHER INFORMATION

Find out about all sorts of science including matter at the Science and Industry Museum!

www.scienceandindustrymuseum.org.uk

Find more science fun in this book!

Discovering Science: What are Materials? by Kay Barnham (Wayland, 2020)

INDEX

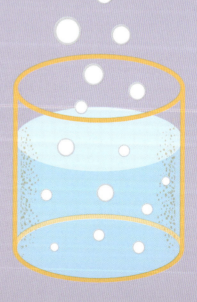